NATIONAL GEOGRAPHIC

PIONEER EDITION

By Dan Hogan

CONTENTS

SEA Monsters

Amazing animals live deep in the ocean. Some are as large as a school bus. Many glow in the dark. Most have sharp teeth. And we keep finding more of them.

By Dan Hogan

Deep-sea octopod

The ocean is deep and dark. What lives there? For years, people did not know. Now scientists are finding out. How?

They use **submersibles,** or subs. Subs can travel to the bottom of the ocean. They have cameras. They take pictures of deep-sea animals. These pictures let scientists see life on the ocean floor.

Scientists also use nets to learn about deep-sea animals. Sometimes scientists find animals no one has seen before. The animals help people understand life in the ocean.

Tough Neighborhood

Living deep in the ocean is not easy. Why? The water is very cold. It can be just above freezing.

It is dark too. Sunlight cannot reach deep areas of the ocean. At about 3,000 feet, the ocean gets totally dark. That is just part of the way down. The deepest place in the ocean is more than 35,000 feet deep!

Deep-sea animals are able to live in the cold, dark water. But the ocean has other dangers—hungry creatures.

The Food Chain

Animals have to eat. Some eat plants. Yet plants are rare in the deep sea. Animals there must eat meat.

This means that deep-sea creatures have two big jobs. They need to find animals to eat, or **prey.** They also have to stay safe from **predators.** Those are the animals that eat prey.

Put predators and prey together and you have a **food chain.** This is a series of animals that eat one another. For example, a shrimp may be eaten by a fish. The fish may be eaten by a giant squid.

Surprise! *This vampire squid looks like an easy meal. It is not. It protects itself with sharp hooks under its arms.*

Strange Creatures. *This sea cucumber lives deep in the ocean.*

Well Armed. *This giant squid has strong arms. Its arms can rip prey apart.*

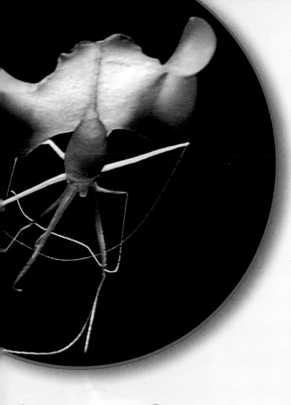

Lights in the Dark

Some animals have an exciting way to catch prey. They glow in the dark.

These animals have special organs, or body parts. The organs make chemicals that glow. Scientists have a name for this ability to glow. They call it **bioluminescence** (by oh loo muh NESS entz). You may have seen it in fireflies.

Bioluminescence helps some deep-sea animals find a meal. Take the dragonfish. This animal has glowing organs under its eyes. It uses them like flashlights to hunt prey.

Glowing in the dark ocean can be risky, though. The lights may catch the eye of a giant squid.

Big Discovery

Giant squid are some of the largest animals in the ocean. Getting noticed by a giant squid is a really bad idea.

Not long ago, scientists found a giant squid that no one had seen before *(left)*. It has eight arms. It is the size of a giraffe.

The squid does not swim like other giant squid. Most squid have a body part called a funnel. They shoot water out of the funnel to swim.

However, this giant squid does not have a funnel. It flaps its fins to swim.

The giant squid was an amazing discovery. Are there more animals to discover in the deep? What might they look like? Future explorers may find the answers.

Wordwise

bioluminescence: ability to make light
food chain: series of animals that eat one another
predator: animal that eats other animals
prey: animal eaten by another animal
submersible: underwater craft

Deep-SEA Dive

Ψhat lives within the ocean? Find out by exploring this picture. It shows a slice of the ocean.

Do you see white or yellow dots on some fish? These stand for bioluminescence, or light created by living things.

The circle (3) gives a close-up view. It shows tiny ocean creatures. They live about 900 feet down in the ocean. The sea cucumber (14) lives more than 13,000 feet down!

1 Flying Fish   8 Giant Squid

2 Mackerel   9 Anglerfish

3 Close-up View   10 Octopod

4 Hatchetfish   11 Gulper Eel

5 Lantern Fish   12 Rattail Fish

6 Viperfish   13 Brittle Star

7 Cyclothone   14 Sea Cucumber

Note: Animals are not drawn to scale.

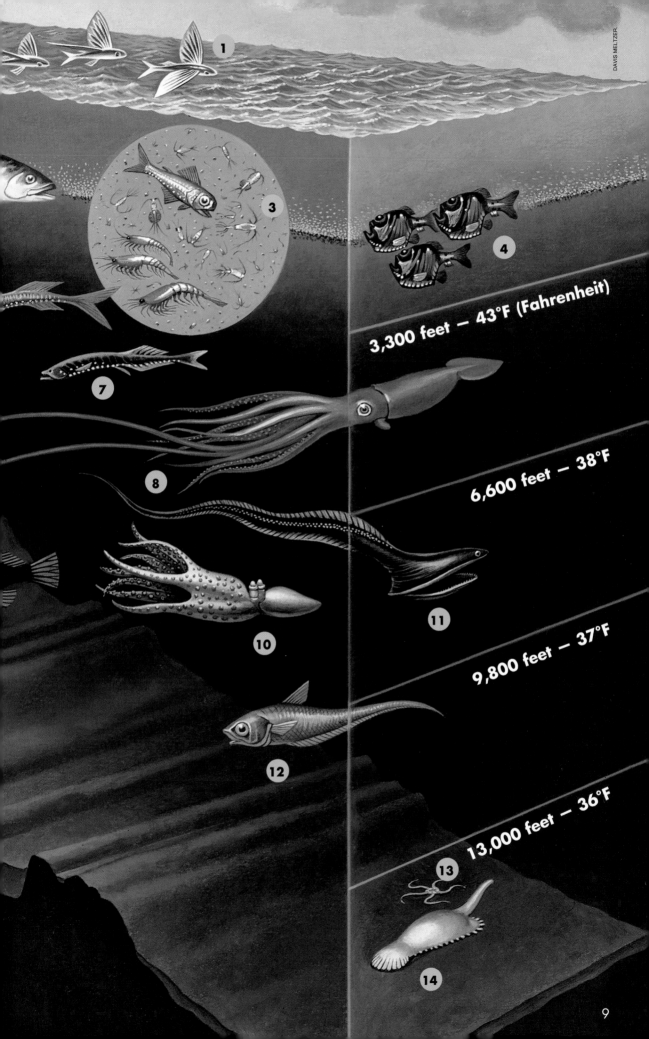

3,300 feet — 43°F (Fahrenheit)

6,600 feet — 38°F

9,800 feet — 37°F

13,000 feet — 36°F

Explore the Seafloor

Animals are not the only things that scientists study in the ocean. They also study the features of the seafloor. Some are similar to those found on dry land. What features do you recognize?

NORTH AMERICA

1

2

Puerto Rico Trench

Mid-Atlantic

ATLANTIC OCEAN

PACIFIC OCEAN

SOUTH AMERICA

Peru-Chile Trench

Braz. Basin

Argentine Basin

1 Seamounts are volcanoes that rise from the seafloor. Some rise 13,000 feet above the bottom of the ocean.

2 Mid–ocean ridges are chains of mountains that run through the ocean. The Mid–Atlantic Ridge is 37,000 miles long.

3 Abyssal plains are the flat areas on either side of the mid–ocean ridges. These areas are covered with sediments.

4 The continental margin borders each continent. At its outer edge, the continental margin can be nearly 6,500 feet deep.

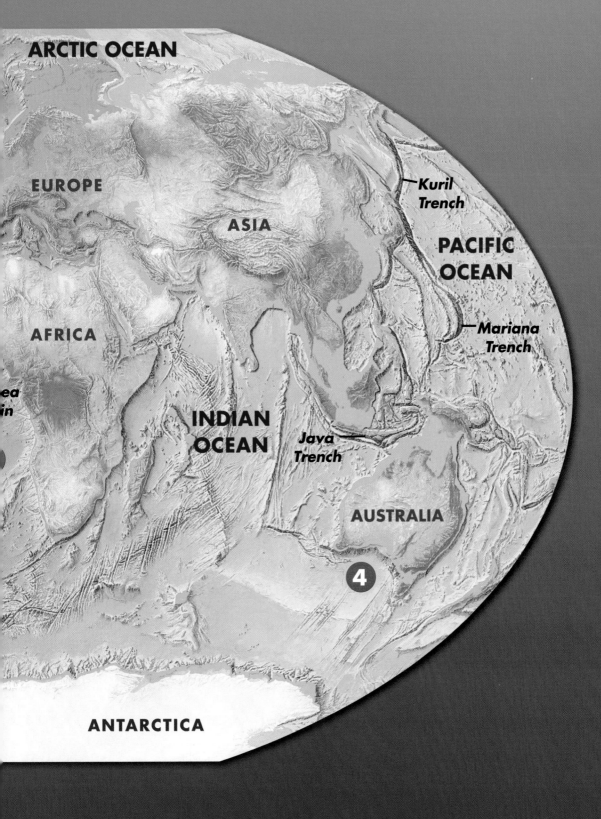

ARCTIC OCEAN

EUROPE

ASIA

Kuril Trench

PACIFIC OCEAN

AFRICA

Mariana Trench

ea in

INDIAN OCEAN

Java Trench

AUSTRALIA

4

ANTARCTICA

The Deep Sea

Dive in to see what you learned about the deep ocean.

1 How do scientists study the ocean?

2 Why is the deep sea a tough place to live?

3 What is a predator?

4 Is a predator ever prey? Explain.

5 What is bioluminescence? How can it help animals find food in the deep ocean?